To the Patron Saint
of Wayward Daughters

To the Patron Saint
of Wayward Daughters

Poems by

Laura Sobbott Ross

© 2021 Laura Sobbott Ross. All rights reserved.
This material may not be reproduced in any form, published,
reprinted, recorded, performed, broadcast,
rewritten or redistributed without
the explicit permission of Laura Sobbott Ross.
All such actions are strictly prohibited by law.

Cover design by Shay Culligan
Cover art by Catrin Welz-Stein

ISBN: 978-1-63980-076-6

Kelsay Books
502 South 1040 East, A-119
American Fork, Utah 84003
Kelsaybooks.com

In memory of the one
whose name was both
a flower and a place
where flowers grow wild,

and to the one, awake,
with islands in her blood.

Acknowledgments

I'm grateful to the editors of the following publications in which these poems first appeared, some in slightly different form:

Albatross: Urchin; *Arkansas Review:* The River; *Babel Fruit:* On Front Street, Philipsburg; *Blackbird:* The Study of Tragedy; *Canary:* Snorkeling in Bonaire; *Clapboard House:* A Prayer for Those at the Edge of the Road; *Coldnoon:* An Island is No Place for a Cat; Floating Past the Orange House in Amalfi; Looking Up, We Marvel; Fish in a Market in Genoa; Côte d'Azur; Ode to Barcelona; *DMQ Review:* Woman Struck by Lightning during Surprise Marriage Proposal; *Dos Passos Review:* She Speaks in Maps; *Driftwood Review:* Boys at the Roller Rink; *Earthshine:* To the Patron Saint of Wayward Daughters; *Glass:* On Saturday Nights She Dances Alone in her Room— the Walls a Shade of Blue-Green called Belize; *JMWW:* Girls at Night on a Beach; *Kestrel:* Ode to Ira-Lee; Wine with Everything was What I Said; *The Ledge:* Skinny Dipping in the Ocean at Age Fifty; *Loch Haven Review:* Girls Born of Water Signs; *New Mexico Poetry Review*: Woman Falls to her Death while Chasing a Feather; *New Orleans Review:* Living Next Door to the Meteorologist; *Ottawa Arts Review:* You Always Had a Gypsy Heart; *Painted Bride Quarterly:* Bora-Bora; Déjà Vu; *The Pedestal:* The Mermaid Who Loves Land Animals; *Permafrost:* Her Mother Walked Naked into the Room; *Pinyon:* Eden and Algebra; *Requited:* Trampolining; *Ruminate:* Mount Pilatus; *San Pedro River Review:* Falling Asleep on Route 15 in Virginia; *South Florida Poetry Journal:* Were They Skates or Rays?; *Split Rock Review:* She Would Remember the Birds; *Terrain.org:* Sixteen Miles from Buffalo, Wyoming; *The Wayfarer:* Coyotes; *Visitant:* A Small Gold Ottoman; A Walk through the Neighborhood before Nightfall.

"To the Patron Saint of Wayward Daughters" won a Merit Award in the International Poetry Contest for the Atlanta Review.

"Skinny Dipping in the Ocean at Age Fifty" won First Place in The Ledge Poetry Contest.

"Girls Born of Water Signs," The Mermaid Who Loves Land Animals," "Urchin," "Woman Falls to her Death while Chasing a Feather," and "Sixteen Miles Outside of Buffalo, Wyoming" were first published in the chapbook "A Tiny Hunger" by YellowJacket Press.

"Coyotes," "A Prayer for Those at the Edge of the Road," and "A Walk through the Neighborhood before Nightfall" were first published in the book "The Trees Will Remain" by Bell Ring Books.

"When Farrah's Hair Fell to Earth" refers to Farrah Fawcett's chemotherapy treatment for cancer.

"You Always Had a Gypsy Heart" is in memory of Ginger Meadows.

"Woman Falls to her Death while Chasing a Feather," and "Woman Struck by Lightning during Surprise Marriage Proposal" were inspired by news reports of actual events.

Special thanks for the fine fellowship at First Friday Writing Group of Lake County, Florida. Thank you to Jim Steele for your buoyant encouragement. Thank you to Gianna Russo and to John Hughes for your enthusiastic support and kind words. Finally, thank you to the lion-hearted women in my life willing to live their truths.

Contents

To the Patron Saint of Wayward Daughters   15

I.

Body of Water

Girls at Night on a Beach	21
When She Saw the Ocean for the First Time	22
You Held the Compass	23
Venezuela	25
In Curaçao, I Became a Fish	27

Continental Drift

A Small Gold Ottoman	31
Her Mother Walked Naked into the Room	33
Conjuring Venus & Other Siren Songs	35
Boys at the Roller Rink	38
Eden and Algebra	39
The Good Girls	40
The River	42
Ode to Ira-Lee	43
Wine with Everything Was What I Said	45

Requiem

You Always Had a Gypsy Heart	49
Death by Crocodile	51
The Study of Tragedy	53
She Would Remember the Birds	55

Falling Asleep on Route 15 in Virginia	56
When Farrah's Hair Fell to Earth	57
Living Next Door to the Meteorologist	59
I Could Have Gone to Cartagena	60
Girls Born of Water Signs	62
Death of a Twin	63
Meditation on the Night	67

II.

The Graces and the Sirens

Flying	73
Mount Pilatus	74
Looking Up, We Marvel	75
Woman Falls to her Death while Chasing a Feather	76
Fish in a Market in Genoa	77
Snorkeling in Bonaire	78
Ode to Barcelona	79
Côte d'Azur	81
An Island is No Place for a Cat	83
Turning Thirty-Three on Saint Lucia	84
On Front Street, Philipsburg	86
Bora-Bora	87

Confluence

Daughter	91
Were They Skates or Rays?	93
The Mermaid Who Loves Land Animals	94

On Saturday Nights She Dances Alone in her Room—the Walls, a Shade of Blue-Green Called *Belize*	96
A Prayer for Those at the Edge of the Road	97
Trampolining	99
Hannah	100
Missing the Missing Girl	102

Vespers

Woman Struck by Lightning during Surprise Marriage Proposal	107
Sixteen Miles from Buffalo, Wyoming	108
A Walk through the Neighborhood before Nightfall	109
Coyotes	110
Déjà Vu	112
Skinny Dipping in the Ocean at Age Fifty	113
Meet my Anxiety	114
Heart	116
Urchin	119
Floating Past the Orange House in Amalfi	120
She Speaks in Maps	122

the Graces and Sirens, glide with linked hands over life.
—Jean Paul Richter

To the Patron Saint of Wayward Daughters

Remember, Sister, how the ocean was her first love—
a tattered hemline skirting sand, the hard shove
of the moon? Hers was a baptism of salt and sinew
and undertow. That's when we discovered she floats,
unspooling me at the edge where I waved her back,
mother-cord looped around her slippery ankle.

I am still without a net, you see. Mercy,
but it's taken me some time to gather a rosary
of baby teeth from beneath pillows humid
with the small breath of dreams. Did I mention
how she surfaces from time to time like a hallelujah?
Her toenails painted in abalone or the asphalt pitch
of balding treads. In her rearview mirror, one eye
precisely inked in ebony. The other, a compass
flailing. *Those alms,* she admonishes, *speak of nothing*

but wind. Or was that you, Sister? Wasn't that you?
Tell me, can you spot her from your God-perch,
your vast heart rolled out—a sticky field of benedictions,
your harp-stung fingers shuffling the stems
to croon a litany. What I meant to confess is
if I had an anecdote for the world and its random cruelties,
I would have spooned it into her mouth like angel

food cake, like armor. Little girl with her plastic purse
and dandelion sun, ghosted into a drift of porous stars.
Her dimpled cheek, a match strike. Throb is a cadence,
don't you think? Even the dusty moths scorch their way
toward machined light; wings, another language
meant to be cindered. O Sister, obtain for me the grace

to be tender when combing out the clouds tangled
in her hair, patient, while unpuzzling the graffiti
still wet beside the gate rusted wide. She's right—
inertia hurts. I'll search for you both in the incense
of windchimes. At your altar, please accept this
fistful of kite streamers. They're all I've got.
Praise song for the fine arc of yearning. Amen
to gravity. To those civilized trails of breadcrumbs
in a fairytale wood. To the stubborn foothold of hunger.

I.

Body of Water

Girls at Night on a Beach

Did you know those grains of sand
when magnified look like charms,
a sorceress's spilled cache—
scarabs & crystals & crumbled bits of amulet,
a broken kaleidoscope glittering the hemlines
of girls who don't tilt toward the light,
but ache for the horizon instead.
It's the sound of their voices I remember,
a current diffused by the ocean's soft prattle.
Flashlights swinging ribbons
that chased ghost crabs sideways
into coves. What is light anyway,
but a form made malleable by darkness,
an inversion of elements,
and did I mention the windchimes
clattering in capiz shells & sea glass
to lantern them home,
or the stars, how they glimmered—
small cogs fevered and pinioned in a night
so tender it could have been a mist?

When She Saw the Ocean for the First Time

it frothed and tumbled my mother
back out with cones and spirals
and ridged bits cupped like sequins
salt-washed of their shine.
On her skin, grains of sand
arranged themselves in braille nodes
and wrote things like *wanderlust*
and *cobblestones, gondolas* and *spires*.

Her hemline wrung heavy
and the compass beneath her tongue
un-obligating its due north bearing
down because you could say
even constellations change hemispheres.
Lottie-Mae's parents driving them back home
to Mississippi along Florida's Gulf Coast,
till its frilled blue edge was a blur.

Naples was lovely, my mother
already writing in her girlish hand,
while a whelk shell she'd stashed away
was held to her ear and sighed of duomos
and lemon trees and smart chiffon scarves
to be worn while whipping around hairpin curves
of inclines that would lead back to the sea.

You Held the Compass

that divided mangroves, gridlines locking
into place between feral coordinates
starting with Amazon, Andes.
The perfect latitude of the equator,
a bearing line just off the page.

The chant of war still distant in your head,
your boots damp with araguaney petals.
The two-hour siestas must have seemed
so decadent, and yet, the heat.

Soon roads sprawled toward oil rigs.
Money mailed back to the States
neatly tallied in the register of solitary years.
Your sacraments offered in no less
than 18-karat Venezuelan gold
when my mother arrived,
undoing the *Belle* from her name
and eying the mountains, one silhouette,
green and wild, rising from another.

All you'd needed were your cedulas to cross
other borders; the Atlantic and Pacific Oceans
close enough for you to have made a choice.
You divided your dilemmas into two sides
of a page, my mother said, pros and cons,
calculated into reason. When it comes to love,
there is no such thing as precision. No perfect line
segment to bear the incalculable weight of it,

despite all the sensibilities a civil engineer
could muster, Catholic, from New Jersey,
who drove a convertible along Lago de Maracaibo
to the Caribbean Sea with a diamond ring
from Tiffany's. At the blue rim, a gasp—
no, not the tide. She'd said yes, hadn't she?

Venezuela

The name itself, a kingdom
brambled over in exotics,
where fish & birds read like orchids,
and an oil-flat sea's gone dull
beside a land possessed of its own
drumbeat. After all, Amazon
sounds more tribal than rivered.

Venezuela, its new language
an assignation of pleasantries,
and even color. *Gracias. Azul.*
It was all I could do as a child to count
in newly named values. *Oleander,*
my mother said, meaning danger.
It's the gravity, she'd say, handing me
a comb. Venezuela on a map
was a cluster of grapes inside
a larger cluster of grapes—
that southern continent, feral & hemispheric.

Nat King Cole crooned from a needle
threading my father's album on the turntable.
A circle un-brailling inward
until it bumped a shoreline of static.
Whole notes opening in concentricity.
Magnético. That was Venezuela.

Rain fell in curtains that cleaved glass
puddles from streets. Black flies
leaving ripples and chewing our calves.
What was the equator anyway,

but a line between ourselves looking up
and the mirrored sky, the same template
of tree and cloud, the same rainbow
hoisted like a banner from a distant fiesta.
Only here, in Venezuela, iguanas
dragoned casually beneath coconut palms,
and the thick rot of frogs plastered the gullies.
Sun, a filigree loose across terrazzo.

Look up. You could bless yourself
on the Southern Cross between
the monkey bars. Whirlwinds reversing.
Epicentro. Every ceiling revolving
in fan blades—the slow tick
of shadow and stir. Always.
Even while you slept. *Be careful*

said the mothers to the fathers,
home for siestas and lifting us children,
combed and giddy, into the current.
Roll your tongue when you say
tierra; yes, it means earth, niñas,
but look how beautiful the swirl
of both hemispheres of stars.

In Curaçao, I Became a Fish

No one saw the tide take me.
One moment I was belly-deep in it,
and then curled inside

a vortex & too young to know
I should have panicked.
Portal, the eyewall of a current

snug enough to accommodate
a small girl. Transience,
the perfect name for a shade of

malleable pink, as in eggshell
broken and cobbled, as in
the shoreline I was undoing

one wet fistful at a time.
Heaven was a turquoise realm
reeling in a vista opposite

of lounge chairs and Coppertone.
I was sure of it. I was five
and didn't know how to say—

Let me let go.

Continental Drift

Your body will collide with earth, and you will bear witness.
—Mark Jenkins

A Small Gold Ottoman

in memory of my father

I wanted you to put it on
my back so I could turtle
through the room on my
hands and knees like any
child might, my bones full
of frolic despite the weight
of your doctor's prognosis.
I wanted you to put it on
my back so I could house
our house of grief in a shell
of top-stitched harvest gold
vinyl and upholstery foam,
so I could carry it like a
cartoon character would—
tongue out in concentration,
reptilian clown in blonde
bangs un-acclimating her
blood to the temperature
of the room. *Why can't you
lift it, why can't you lift it?*
I wanted to shout and beat
my fists against your ribs
until you saw me—small,
soft body gone awkward
with your displacement,
the sudden paradigm of
ceilings & doors. Your bed,
a grave in the living room,
as if cancer was just a cruel
un-armoring, as if the only
point of gravity I needed was

the one in which a small gold
ottoman hung in the balance.

Her Mother Walked Naked into the Room

We hovered at miniature rooms
of the Tudor house where we rearranged
the furniture, defining spaces
with the penchants of our girl hands.
Did I mention the clawfoot tub
by the hearth of birch twigs
or the kitchen sink at the balcony rail?

Above the roofline, the naked woman,
brief and startling, sliding into her robe.
At night, I coveted that dollhouse,
shingle & shutter, every perfectly
scaled amenity. From the open sashes

of its windows, trees became redwoods,
the bed, a chenille plateau without seasons,
and her mother's breasts, moons
eclipsed with small pink planets—
shadows thrown from our suburbia
of tiny hinges & postcard sized rugs.

The scientific names for genitalia
sounded like constellations,
words we'd gasped & giggled over.
The stairs between stories, a curve
sweeping in such small increments,
we could take them a hundred times

a day with just our fingers. We slid
tiny tins into a matchbox sized oven,
and opened lace curtains to the boxed reds
of geraniums while we whispered of breasts
still latent on the flat horizons of our ribcages.
Breasts, that would rise radiant and disquieted
from our flesh the way wings do.

Conjuring Venus & Other Siren Songs

Wanna-be wallflower, selective mute, color-me-gray—
I studied beauty from the back of the classroom. Sapphire
on my tongue, the cells behind the unremarkable shade
of my eyes, tactile & faceting. I pretended I knew

*\~

no answers. My Barbie wore leopard trimmed
gold Lycra, had push-pin earrings, and an agenda.
Ken, with his bad knees, sprawled shotgun
in her idling pink convertible. Voodoo?
No. Potion & spell—here's what I remember:
a Luna moth on my windowsill, hopscotch,
angelfish, and across the Ouija board, a favor
from a wedding—candy-coated almonds
scattered and crackling like sprouted seeds.
Beneath my pillow, a bee stung me in my sleep.

*\~

My mother baked me a cake with a girl inside of it,
not really a girl, but a doll whose wide eyes burned
beyond her frilled stasis of pink and white.
Was she wearing a foothold piped in sugar paste
roses or a skirt? Nothing meant for dancing.
Just a girl made lighter by what consumed her.

*\~

In Greek Mythology class, I chose Venus, of course.
Goddess of hair & wind chimes & sea foam.
I dreamed I was made of thorns, and inside
a plastic ring box, I kept a dried seahorse,

exquisite and primitive as a fossil—
hippocampus, amygdala, a universe
of gray matter assimilating. The chant:

    *\~

I want. I want to be. I want to be pretty.
exchanged with wet pennies, first stars, thistle,
smoke & birthday candles. Every night, the same
dark, follicled horizon. The moon, an ovum released.
Craving takes the shape of a rib, hollow and listing,
and I think a whale's song is the purest recollection
of a place you cannot be. Remote, I was born a water sign.
It's no wonder I saw islands in that inkblot test.

    *\~

I don't know how my teeth grew in straight
despite what was gnarled beneath my skin—
an anxiety that would rattle me in midair
until I wanted to run across every field,
if only open spaces didn't make me feel
so nervous and exposed. The artistic sister,
I painted ghost ships & singular girls in orchards.

    *\~

What I meant to say is *desire.*
What I meant to say is *dormant*
comes in a palette of matte & glossy,
an iridescence on my fingers and hidden
behind foggy eyeglasses on the high school bus.
Those songs on the AM radio pressing against me
like the heat of a slow dance, my first French kiss.

*\\~

Soon enough, one appeared—
a skinny Michelangelo's David
in a silver car with a spoiler and a flame
breathing eagle on the hood.
The apple blossoms thick as Noxzema
that year. And when he kissed me,
fairies crawled out of my hair.
I named myself at last
in a longing whispered from his lips.

Boys at the Roller Rink

The boys at the roller rink
came from the wrong side of town.
They swallowed the oval floor
in strides that never wavered
or sent them spinning
with outstretched fingers
slippery from their own oily scalps,
body odor at least a length or two behind.

Wind in billowy polyester shirttails,
they were often called out for skating too fast,
though the wheels of their rented skates
could be easily stilled in the rim
of rubber matting. It was grace—

theirs, not ours, which made us hide
in the girls' bathroom once an hour
when *free skate* became *couples only*.
A sweaty palmed proclamation
that stirred the mirrored ball in the ceiling
to scatter dizzying sequins across the room.

We were afraid the boys
at the roller rink might ask us
to join them, link their fingers
into ours and wing us
across their roadmap of shadows,
the relentless gravity of hard surfaces,
leaving an ache beyond
any *Three Dog Night* song
played back-to-back.

Maybe we were afraid
they wouldn't ask us anything at all.

Eden and Algebra

Tick-tock, the mathematical term for
minutes passing while being tutored
in algebra; a chime for every nine hundred
beats of the second hand around the face

of the clock. It's not as if I was counting
time, a concept too simple for the matrix
of numbers snaking through a paradise lost,
where Adam and Eve were now x and y,
cursed to redefine the other eternally.

Even the integers were pinioned to a grid—
a linear map of constellations. How uninspiring,
concluded the dominant right lobe of my brain,
a whirling jangle of random connectivities.

What did it matter anyway? I wanted to ask
my algebra tutor, an x widowed of her y,
who must have spent her spare time
feeding dry numbers to adolescents like me,
whose silences increased exponentially.
The piano keys in x's living room gone
dormant of their values of sharps and flats
and allegrettos until someone with a formula
of notes laid hands on them again.

Let's bonfire these textbooks, I wanted to tell her,
I'll light the match and you algorithm some jazz
through the open window. We'll dance
in the ash of numbers, whole and primed,
drifting skyward like wishes. The stars,
asterisks, another expression for multiply.

The Good Girls

always have a pen, or gum, or the answer
to the question the teacher is going to ask.
They will help gather the scattered contents
of someone's purse or loose-leaf notebook
without being asked, the teacher busy
praising the hyperactive boys for a moment
of adequate listening. The good girls love

the color pink. They notice hair and shoes
and fingernail polish and a thousand
unspoken nuances inside a conversation
because they're girls, after all,
and that's what girls do. The grades
they seek in school are attainable—
thorn-shaped A's that leave no red marks.
Expressions and variables left pondered
in the margins because aren't boys better
in math than girls? They'll sign up for it all:
viola lessons, French Club, gymnastics, secretary
of the student council; Saturday mornings,
selling thin mints in a uniform in front of Kroger.
Thank you notes are prompt and handwritten,
their signatures wandering into little flourishes.

The good girls keep their old teddy bears
propped up on their pink bedspreads
and sometimes at night they bite their rage
into those fleece limbs when they think of being
expected to help the eye-rollers again in history class
with a timeline the good girls will write themselves
anyway, because they care, and what a curse it is
to care so much and not be noticed for it, and how
they might portion time with their own longings—

a subtext skewed and snapping beneath
a linear agenda. Because who are they anyway,
but what they wait for, parsed and clinking in a tin cup.
Their own windy hearts walled in a tower
barbed in sweetbriar. And when they do fall
asleep, the good girls don't dream of flying,
but of sorting spoons into nested stacks
or taking tests they hadn't studied for.
Sometimes they dream about finding themselves
naked, of songs crooned into their ears with lyrics
like *flywheel,* like *sweet darlin',* like *opine.*

The River

I was the clerk in sullen black eyeliner,
the one who left notes on your car—
Have a beautiful day.

Thin shouldered seventeen
shrugging off every second thought
like a church dress.

Your cousin asked me out first,
but he was only concerned about my salvation,
while you drove me through the kind of blackness
where you couldn't see your own hand
in front of your face. I wasn't afraid
even when you would stop
to hold some nocturnal creature
spellbound in a beam of light.

We drank Pabst Blue Ribbon by the river.
My mother said you were a tightwad,
that all you ever bought me was an ice cream cone—
a scoop of lemon custard on a Saturday night.
It might as well have been the moon,
dripping down into the marsh ferns,
where we inhaled the heady earth of summer.

Night rushing in like the sound of the river,
blind current locked into precipitous gravity—
wellspring of a distant, indiscernible mouth
at last coming close enough to find my own.

Ode to Ira-Lee

My mother's cousin danced
with a cigarette between her lips—
Maybelline, in a matte pigment
so red it was banned from nature,
all twenty-seven shades of dusk on river,
not even a leaf broadsided by autumn.

No one's moonbeam girl,
the worst thing she ever did
besides having a sassy mouth
with an incisor sharp as a compass arrow,
was to buy a black lace bra
with pointed cups and run away
one September to California.
Her hair flying in the wind across the desert—
land so flat and soft it collected
echoes and cactus roses,
and the tire treads of mercenaries.

Mama, the ocean is the bluest
thing you could ever imagine,

she would have written
dotting her *i's* in astonishment
across the back of a postcard.
Ira-Lee, in a windy scarf and capris,
and a boy, exotic as an earthquake,
sleeveless with a thin moustache
that tasted of sea salt and spearmint.

The radio set to Jerry Lee
from Ferriday, back home,
and a tray of ice cubes going white
in a Frigidaire where she kept
a small jar of eye cream
heirloom tomatoes, bottles of cola.
Through the windows,
a purple jacaranda tree
hissing with bees, and the edge
of the sea. Lord, a whole latitude
so rude and beautifully wrecked.
All that perfect light.

Wine with Everything Was What I Said

when someone would ask me
for the color of my lipstick.
I loved the way it made me feel
like a mad queen issuing a proclamation—

Wine with Everything and enough
roasted squab for all the rowdy villagers.
A festival of plums & harlequin roses—
that color, I mean, the way it never bled
in betrayal across my teeth. *Amative*—

(disposed to love), the gist of a shade
too kitten-heeled and pearly for me,
a shimmer lifted away by the wind
while riding on the back of an older boy's
motorcycle when you were supposed to
be home babysitting your younger brother.

Mars Rising, a chroma too atmospheric
not to leave what looked like a trail of blood
across throats and earlobes, and let me just say
Desire Was a Blue-Eyed Man, silky & humid,
a taste that really left me wanting
to be kissed down there by the river
before I learned *Crush* was a color
that meant avalanche, matte and opaque,

too heavy for a girl revved up on Revlon,
a girl too impractical to sustain
the momentum of anything but dancing,
who thought there was nothing more
hypnotic than moonlight darkening the hollows
of a man's cheekbones. I tried them all—

by that I mean the lipstick shades, of course—
the orchids and the mochas and the corals,
the lacquered, the frosted,
the ticklish feather coats of glossy nudes,
the amber-golds and apricots—all
imprints ghosting from goblets raised
in the palette cleansing light
between him and him and him.
Wine with Everything clinging to the rim.

Requiem

You Always Had a Gypsy Heart

I came to your funeral smelling of vodka,
residual fumes of a plane
I was sure would fall from the sky—
not willing to believe that one of us
could go without the other.

The pastor said in the eulogy
that you could be feisty,
and we had all smiled unexpectedly.
Your eyes were as blue as moonstones,
I always thought. Dark Irish,
you had told the curious, when asked.

Your last letter arrived on your birthday.
You said you were happy again—
it was summer in Sydney, and you
were going to Perth to float up the coast.
Hadn't I just called you a year before,
sunburned on a balcony in San Juan,
to sing *Happy Birthday* over an ocean
that railed like a raucous celebration?

You always had a gypsy heart.
I recognized it at the edge of the Blue Ridge—
mountains that lay around us in repose
like muses long given up their siren songs,
a paunchy silhouette of hip and bosom,
an earth we could almost lean into.
Her mossy breath, both judgement and lullaby.

Hadn't we tried to shake the spell
of valleys and high school boys?
Bell bottoms caught in bicycle chains
and sharing moons like highway tolls,
waiting for fate to choose which one of us to go.

Death by Crocodile

*In memory of my friend, Ginger Meadows, who was killed
by a crocodile in 1987 at King's Cascades in Northwestern Australia.*

Yeah, it's an angry title,
but isn't it what you want to hear?
By that, I mean those of you
who stand wide-eyed at her shrine.
What are you hoping for?
See the toothbrush and the rosebud buckle?
The limpet from her pocket,
a brittle star—an asterisk denoting a shriek.

It's true. It's how she died.
An X on a map near a waterfall
in Darwin where a tree now grows
hard against the outflow.
Tell me, what was she like?

asks one of you, never.
Here's something about her
you couldn't forget, I whisper,
drawing you in. We are lapped
in brackish water, picking swamp grass
from our flesh. You shiver.

It was her eyes, I tell you, eyes shot through
with the bluest light you can imagine.
Eyes that could conjure a sudden current.
(There is only the sound of a surge eddying.)
*Wasn't she wearing a bikini
when it happened?*
one of you dares to ask, leaning in.
I mean, who dies like that, right?

I conspire in hisses. She was beautiful.
Is that what you want to know?
A full-on Fay Wray in the grips of a primal beast.
Do you want me to detail the thrashing of her torso?
The despair in the arc of her wrists? Did you know

she loved top shelf margaritas and the underdog?
That her hair was humid, but her scent was cactus rose.
That she kept a poster of Dennis Wilson on her wall
and collected keys and geographies and left
mascara on my mother's tea towels. Give me back
her watercolor brushes, you bastards,
her father's yard of daffodils by the highway,
the way she laughed like she was choking.

You are a breathless lot, aren't you?
Go home.
There's no body to recoil from,
no sand to sift for fragments
of mercury and bone.
Oh, wait. Look. Here's a trinket—

she'd had a premonition,
dreamt of crabs pinching at her belly,
of sea urchins tangled in drifts of her hair,
her lungs wrung with dark water.
She'd cried when she told me about it,
and by tears, I mean a bloodletting
in the bluest blue—write this down, witnesses—
in the bluest blue you can possibly imagine.

The Study of Tragedy

We can't help but stir the ashes, finger
the relics, the proofed bits of minutia
improvised into legacy—the missing girl's
last drink, a cherry vodka sour.
The box of long-stemmed roses
by the door wicking a speck of blood.
Is it too much to remember the one

abducted on her way to school
had a check in her pocket to buy a lamb,
or the one who was strangled
left the window open that night
because she'd burned the meatloaf?

We can pick through the crumbs
trailing into the troll-dark forest,
no one will be following them back home—
the shoe by the bridge, the spent cigarette,
the button, the handprint, the hair.

We want to reassure ourselves
there was no ambush, that no one was sleeping
when the stranger stealthed into her bedroom.
We'd like to believe in inklings, patterns
of fate more than footprints in snow,
or a pillow used as a weapon.

Read the words in the diary of the dead
backwards this time. Were there signs
of a struggle? Hadn't she sensed someone
was watching? Were her dreams about falling?

Look deeper at the photo, through the tea leaves
of the iris of the eye, past the pupil's black eclipse,
into the sea-grassy current of synapse, sphincter, cilia,
the hair-trigger neurons synchronized to snap shut,
the last cell still warm and scribed in smoke.

She Would Remember the Birds

My mother worries over dark water
and snow. It must be the way
both transform the familiar.
Peril—a word pretty enough

to describe the glittery encasement
of winter. Erasure in a slaughter
of cloud-sift, anxiety no less defined
by clot and smatter, sharp edges
going deeper. Beneath a warm spotlight,

my mother would remember the birds,
the same ones that stunned themselves
against our summer windows,
soft beating hearts with addled wings.
Despite the menagerie of ice,
they would feast on suet and seed.
Gathering, like my mother's own dark flock
of thoughts at night on the same old roost.

But what else could you do in a house
full of sons and a wayward daughter?

Children who would turn in opposing compass points
far beyond the landscape's fragile keeping.
Children, my mother would recall,
who'd left their angels flapping in the drifts,
and rode the slippery hills face first on waxed blades.

Falling Asleep on Route 15 in Virginia

Buckingham was the place we might have died,
blonde lovers sleeping in a wayward Impala.
The route home, a droning gray
threading the lull of rural darkness. Drifting
after me, after beers in a fraternity basement,
you'd crossed the yellow line.
Low-swept branches held to us
like brittle hooks at the edge of a precipice.
The back tires paused on a curve in the highway,
gearshift still in drive, dashboard lit and humming.
Soon frost would fall around the warm cloud of exhaust,
the dogwoods and the redbuds dormant in this kingdom
of slumber, this hushed cadence of breathing unaware.
But we woke instead. We woke to random faces
peering into the glass, aquarium-like, tapping out:
hey-are-you-okay-in-there, startling at the way
our eyes flew open, our pale forms shouldering upright,
trailing a plume of exhaust and kudzu into the night.

When Farrah's Hair Fell to Earth

It was all humid heat and wind
defying helixes of hair sprung
from curling rods smoldering
beside bathroom sinks.
Every girl wanted wings

like Farrah's—
angled layers pressed into waves
that crested and fell by noon,
weakening like the ozone
beneath a shellacking of Aqua Net.

Iconic, the way she seemed to jiggle
her mane and every filament settled
into a hush that preserved an era
in pomade, spray wax, hair cream.

Decades later, Farrah's hair
would fall to earth in golden shivers
after she'd traded it for a miracle.
On her altar, each candlewick's
flaxen flame point snuffed out
by a cellular saturation that could
humanize even television goddesses.

Now, someone claims to be selling it
in clipped lengths, suggesting
the owner could clone Farrah,
use the genetic code pillared inside
each strand of champagne blonde—

Farrah rising from the foam
of her own radiant waves,
golden, beaming, windblown as Venus.

Living Next Door to the Meteorologist

His door would open when I arrived at mine,
click of key to lock so much easier to discern
than the yin & yang of satellite jet streams.
Eyeglasses, humid. Hair—Einstein-wild.
He would always act surprised to see me.

I never asked him for a forecast,
although I wondered about a man
who could read the braille of clouds,
who could predict the colliding thresholds
of highs & lows. Walls so thin between

us, I could hear him yawn at night.
It wouldn't have taken much for him to know
I already had a lover—boots on the stairwell,
scent of cigarette; our voices, an undulating
atmosphere, a bead of mercury in flux.
Did he hear me coo at my cat in the window,
her gold eyes fixed on the horizon?

It would have been impolite of me to ask
why he wanted my address when I said
I was moving to Florida. Our thumbprints,
swirled hurricanes in the ocean on a map.
Here, I told him, pointing at the heart

of the peninsula, a destination charted between
latitudes & magnetic poles. *Snowlessness,*
my own barometric term, gradients and currents
that ebbed me south. I never wrote him back,
read with fleeting curiosity his letters penned
in aching plain-speak—hindsight, a theorem
that never works for weather or intention.

I Could Have Gone to Cartagena

Seven hundred miles from the midline.
Heat. Everything, a color—
braille for the living eye.
Lagoon, for example, a single node
eddying into every tincture of blue.

Pero, no habla español, señor,
I told the hiring manager.
No hay problema, he shot back.

African soul, Catholic yoke, Colonial architecture—
arcs and struts and balustrades,
walls frescoed in every flavor of popsicle,
even the ones you didn't know existed—
gulupa, guava, zapote, mangosteen.
Bougainvillea, an exclamation too bawdy
for cathedrals, plazas of cobblestone and pigeon.
This is what old shade smells like.
This is what fresh tamarind juice and rum taste like.

Ceiling fans ticking while I wrote
letters home from a rented room.
What's there, anyway, someone might have asked.

How about emeralds laid bare and waiting
for hooks and prongs, men
with eyes the color of black olives,
the speculators with their mangos & baskets & mochilas?
Me, redefining myself in another

language, latitude, architecture. I hesitated.
Maybe loneliness would follow me in like weather.
Something unprecedented shuttering the natives,
something to be wrung from what lay drying
across the saturated pigments of their balcony rails.

I trembled while Cartagena waited for me,
oiled and sandaled beneath her billowing skirts.
She shuffled her deck of cards and fanned them out
for me to choose what she would reveal about me—
an interpretation already loose on her tongue.

Girls Born of Water Signs

If they had looked into our palms,
those men with fingers cold
as a dew point on a beer bottle,
they might have seen the tracery of tides,

as if holding an egg with a fissured shell.
Weren't we, the girls born of water signs,
supposed to be blessed with intricate
sensitivities? We laughed,

my Pisces friend and me, at a guy
with his tie in his plastic cup of beer
when he asked us both out for seafood.
Saturday night, a moonless swim

between the bodies and the bar,
its concrete floor littered with oyster shells.
Fishnet swags throwing shadows across
strangers' faces who almost came close enough.

A friend, born the same week of November,
ruled out the boys of earth and fire and air,
who offered morning boat rides on the river,
the compromises of sun and wind.

Oh, how I wanted to take them at their word,
shake the neon from my hair,
stand on the shore with my skin burning,
thump of pearl between my ribs.

Death of a Twin

in memory of M.& E.

eh' ad
Genesis. Brothers born
the Year of the Dragon,
under the sign of twins—
Gemini, in Jerusalem, a city again,
not much older than a boy.
One twin holding the ankle
of the other at birth
like Jacob & Esau?

shtaim
In that shared temple
of your mother's womb,
you were not a map dividing,
but a geography duplicating.
An eclipse undone—the first
lucent rib, jaws bobbing upright,
limbs twitching to separate currents.

schalosh
Across hemispheres, years—another June,
another reckoning. You & me,
a shared and magnetizing heat.
As children, we had learned to write
our alphabets from opposing margins.
The same axis realigning
the moment our itinerant currents
wrenched us together.

arba
In the naked light
of your room I came
to feel beautiful. Compass
at my marrow stilling
beside your soldier skin—
north star in a constellation of scars,
lodestone of bullet & lullaby.
Two sides of the same
globe; religion, history, language
distilled to a singular Psalm
of desire. *Don't close your eyes,*
you whispered, your mouth everywhere.

chamesh
Love is a charge more annihilative than war.
Your brother told me
you had wired underwater bombs to bridges.
There was nothing careful at your house.
The backyard, a floodplain. Oaks shook
and broke into helmeted seed.
A revolver lay loaded on the nightstand,
and lemons with paprika steeped in sunlit jars.
You and I ate them whole, skin and all.
Not too much, bad for the heart,
your brother said. It was crowded then—

shesh
he & you; you & me.

shevah
I broke us, blinked and exhaled.
My name, a prayer
folded inside a wall
on the other side of the world.
Exodus, the highway south
where I dragged the horizon
across state lines into the wind.

schmoneh
Decades later, your ghost rises
from your brother's voice.
You move on the other side
of his mirror, a cleaved mercury.
Or mercy? He tells me what it means
when I dream about you—
your songs at elevator doors,
me with no shoes on, kisses
that transpire like nourishment.
Someone once asked us:
Who would we worship?

tesha
I tell your brother things I wish
I could have said to you before
the sky lay chawed and writhing.
Lamentations. Your half-life
dividing into halves dividing
into halves dividing. How could we

eser
ever share you again?
He weeps when he tells me
how you'd asked him to sing
to you the day you died.
Your connection defying satellites,
lamb's blood and angels,
amnion and atom—
sacred verses lifting from both
sides of the same page.
Words I know
in a language
I would never understand.

Meditation on the Night

I love the beauty of it.
Its great solitude and engulfment.
Saturated,
a word that sounds like being
kissed too many times.

I once tried to ignore it,
to shoo it away
with satellite sound and lamplight.
And wakefulness.
Now I listen.
Am I brave enough?
Am I weary enough?
My ear pressed against it,
where I ready myself for grief,

but find, instead,
the small glass sound of crickets,
the hushed essences
of the day's slaughters and dances,
the smoke and brine of our encampments.
Canticle sounds like an intricate piece of the heart,
but it's just a common praise song.
Tonight, it sings of trains and rivers,
of moths—their wings, a beating cilia
fanning currents inward, while moonlight

is a precision, its own weather,
ancient and mild, a lullaby gone
cellular. Crave, the iron name
for each bone that cages the heart. I think
of the dead, those I kissed, those I wanted

to love me. The stars, a philosophy
reeking light; the sky still
changing hemispheres—
Andromeda, Perseus, Auriga, Cassiopeia—
a continuum of small burnings.

II.

The Graces and the Sirens

Flying

Inching east across
a planet revolving west,
I check the cloudbanks again,
fiercely bruised with weather.
We aren't any more fragile here,
eleven miles or so above the earth
than we are standing on it,
every softness in us still
encapsulated and propelled.

From this tower window,
I promise God to pray for all things
skyward and in transit—
the words themselves, multifold,
while I long for simpler landings.

As a girl, I remember
pinpoints of runway lights—
a blue so alkaline I could feel
my retinas wince.
I dreamt of flying then.
Now, transcending time-zones,
I think of more—
the spooling courses
of ocean, wind, gravity, fate.
The whole sky,
a thronging, humid sphere
held intact by infinite space.

Mount Pilatus

Lake Lucerne, Switzerland

Beneath café umbrellas, patrons sip coffees
from highball glasses, swirls of cream
undisturbed by the current of their lips at the rim.
The Alps, across the baby blue glass of Lake Lucerne,
are a silhouette of fading tinctures, etched & rising.

We keep our carry-on bags close as toddlers
while we wait for our hotel room,
not too jetlagged to be distracted
by diluted blues splattered in flowerbox-brights,
or the crest of limestone that looms above it all—
Mount Pilatus, a legacy of dragons,
of souls' eternal unease. Even the swans
that drift and preen their cloud-thick bodies,
hiss like savages at those who lean in too close
from their midday strolling. Did you know

Pontius Pilate's body is buried on the mountain
and blamed for conjuring drastic weather (and dragons?)
His ghost sealed inside a stone incline where tourists
trek a vertigo of wildflowers and chiming cowbells.
The locals swear Pilate rises every Good Friday
to wash the blood of Christ from his hands.

Does he think about his wife, Claudia, and lament
not heeding her warning, her tactile petition of dreams?
Cloudy, he might have nicknamed her, remembering
how her throat had trembled at his torso,
how the wisps of her hair were a plea against his skin.

Looking Up, We Marvel

at the shattered labyrinth
of the Acropolis, all teeth and rib—
dinosauric relics unpuzzled
into blueprint, myth, weather, war.
After all, this was someone else's
civilization, an elaborate lantern
of friezes and fluted colonnades
meant to a house a girl-flame—
warrior-goddess long gone home
to her owls, every pick and chisel
swinging from a dead man's hands.
Jesus in his time would have
called this place old. Don't pocket
anything. It's bad luck, you see.
Even the smallest sliver can bring
about the evil eye. Nothing but poisonous
oleander thrives in the graveled soil.
Athens, that teeming city encircling
us from every angle, is distilled
to these perfect ruins, to this pilgrimage,
where tourists with our sandaled feet
have polished the marble patches
on the incline into a crude
and slippery monument of awe.

Woman Falls to her Death while Chasing a Feather

Headline from the Telegraph *- Budleigh Salterton, Devon, England*

Was it like her to wander off the trail?
That damn feather at her fingertips,
butterfly-ish, spooling with sea breezes.

No plea could have urged her more
than its spell, conjuring in midair,
scrolled in sky-colored curlicues.

Somewhere beneath her own hands,
she heard the smashed sea inhale,
felt the rasping of beach pebbles,
fat as yeast rolls. Rocking at the brim

of guardrail, that pretty shred of wing—
more delicate than the wild angelica
pressed between her leaves of Psalms,
the abalone shell, or the sea glass beads
small as baby teeth in her silver creamer.

The soft edge of her at last at the soft edge,
she found it rosy as a wall of sunlit sandstone,
insubstantial as the lacy foam of the sea,

the sudden pitch of wind in between,
a regret too slippery to hold her,
holding the feather holding the sky.

Fish in a Market in Genoa

Astonished, is how they died,
one gold eye upright,
sound as a cat's.
Something salty on their tongues,
if they'd had tongues
on which to choke or flail,
and howl into the spaceless space
a last word between them,
the final sheen-on-sheen
spasm of grief or ecstasy.
They are beautiful.
Small rainbowed forgivenesses.
So, this is what dying looks like—
the day's dull, hungry hum
in your portion of a slow-motion sky,
snagged in a sudden terrible tat of current,
the volumetric inverse of an ocean
you can't contain inside your primitive cells,
and so, you tumble, slide, affix
your silver flopping tail to the light.

Snorkeling in Bonaire

Eden Beach

I tip my face into another universe,
                         breathe in. Here,
                 everything has a current—
     hemline of a thin dress in wind,

hushing the howl of tourists & orange awnings.
       Strangers in masks,
             we are careful
                     in our new buoyancy,

       not to bump against one another
as we chase what hovers and flits

    from scale to scale and back
at the shoreline of flat, furred stones,
                   must we surface?

   There's clarity here.
       Blues ebbing into
               deeper blues.

     Aren't we lighter?
      See how we can soar
         above the clutch

of soft corals, keepers of their own
     blooming, the open-mouthed kisses
         of fish. Oh God, I know

the way the limpets don't want to let go.

Ode to Barcelona

I left you too soon, Barcelona,
your stone hillside of petulant angels,
your iron-tatted balconies, your cinnamon
haze, your spires & cannons & crypts.
The sudden flame of bougainvillea,
mouthy and righteous. Everything, a dare.
A whim. A hemline whipping & brambled.

I wanted to dance with you, Barcelona,
your candles gone liquid, your blue
twilight under lace, your tavern wine,
your velvet skirts combed humid
with summer, your red mouth lit
with saffron & clove. That mesmerizing
crooked eyetooth when you laugh.

I wanted to eat with you, Barcelona,
tapas & cava & mocha. Your cityside,
a broken dragon husked and draped
to a whip-blue sea. At the open window,
a sequin catching on a rim so fine it wails.
Truffle. Cuttlefish. Artichoke. Aubergine.
Bobal wicking purple on white linen.

I wanted to walk with you, Barcelona,
along your mosaic curbs of grouted confetti,
your spiral-shell walls of sea-whisper,
your Roman stanchions of blood & pig & sweat.
In your marketplaces, candy-bright produce,
beggars & pickpockets, splays of dawn
colored lilies razored against fortress walls.

And, I wanted to feel you, Barcelona,
your bedsheets and your tambourine moon,
your flamenco tide rattling hulls & shutters,
your wolf & leather scented wind, your stars
sliding hot into grottos. The way the harbor
pivots, lights the column line of date palms,
and opens the soft, willing throats of doves.

Côte d'Azur

Saint-Paul-de-Vence

Bougainvillea could be another word
                        for medieval ghostings—
motet of magenta, plainchant of purple,
it's everywhere— raucous notes
               eclipsing palette-knifed stone.

France smells like linen & eau de civilized
Tuesday afternoons, shop girls in pomade
& rosewater, parchment corners folded
to flag a certain lyric. In this town,

spigots spill cold with piped mountain brooks,
and Chagall lies patiently reverent,
anchored in his grave beneath small stones
                     of purveyors & pilgrims

who've climbed with their living eyes
                         these vines & arches,
those shutters hinged wide to slopes
of cypress and clay tile roofs,
                 the blue horizon of sea.

Every time our guide says *hamlet,*
it sounds like *omelet,* and I think
of fissuring shell, the essence
of tumble & fray purposed on the tip of a fork—
     I'll go left & you go right.

We are apostles on a scavenger hunt:
    sundial, braided garlic, macaroon,
    clay pot of lavender, iron bell, olive tree,
    lace curtain, and rosé. A cat with sunflower
    gold eyes lazes in the gothic fretwork
of shadow & sun, and ignores the artless
       offerings of our hands.

An Island is No Place for a Cat

There's only a boundary of clamor
and sea-hiss, a rock where ripples die,
a wicking salt sheen to be tongued

away, and who knows if cats
can even see the color blue,
discern its striations: sea, mountain, sky.

Some say life originated here on Crete,
a mammalian inception, cell bumping cell
into an abacus of hunger, the first thread

of tabby's spooling stripe, pigment
of calico unbraided into orange, black, & cream.
Millions of mornings later, the same

sun, the same ache of burgeoning
civilization. Olive trees & smoke. Mullet
flailing in nets. Purple blossoms tumbling

wide-mouthed over stone walls,
where cats are curled like fossils
in ancient niches and grottos,

a fish or bird ribbed inside each twitching dream,
so close to our fingers we can almost stroke
the geography of their wild, startled bones.

Turning Thirty-Three on Saint Lucia

God, the valley we'd bounced into—
a perfect clarity, the light
lushly textured in fronds and wind.
Volcanic spires like skyscrapers.
But rainbowed. Chartered and waterfalled.

It was November of trumpetfish.
Of will and willingness.
Of orchid trees and hummingbirds.
Of island boys in braids seeking
tourists to pay them just to look
back at the shore from
their thin painted boats.

You asked me to marry you.
(It would not be the first time.)
You were fearless, and I love that, still
longing to be a mermaid, I snorkeled alone
while you drank beer on the shore,
your shadow buoyant beside me.
At night, the island anchored the moon,
and we sang karaoke with British tourists.
The stars so close we could have
combed them from our hair.
I slid you my secrets, half folded,
and let you let them go in the flame.

Happy Birthday, baby, you said,
and bought me a necklace
from a beachside vendor.
Beads swirled in blues and greens—
a rosary of small earths,

yours & mine, incantations of November:

*mountain, mountain, moon shell, Venus,
nightjar, tamarind, oleander, sea.*

On Front Street, Philipsburg

Saint Martin

Women with hands like mermaids
wave us in—an elegant current
in front of jewelry shops that glint
with glass and facets.

Lookin' don' cost you a thing, baby

the next one will call,
coaxing us with free beer
and Cuban cigars.
Soon enough we are caught
beneath the flame trees,
mesmerized by the gold

breasted finches,
the dark humming-
birds, and malachite
butterflies feasting
there with a raucousness
more distracting
than the croon of enterprise,
and all those merchants
who wait with their gemstones
to be set and spangled and dangled,
and to fracture what is left
of this perfect hungry light.

Bora-Bora

for Doug

We married there, like pirates caught
between the blue chakras of sky & water,
a handful of hungover natives and French tourists
shaking New Year's Eve from the folds of their pareos.

Bonne Annee! They toasted us. Dancing,
a tide etched in sand. Petal-strung, we twisted
our new gold bands into torchlight & promises
big enough to stretch back across any ocean.
Love, a sugared rim we shared in sips—
every edge garnished in hibiscus, sunburn, pineapple.

Back at our tiki hut—wedged on stilts
into confetti clouds of fish, oysters lipping black pearls—
the moray eel we'd spotted earlier.
His prehistoric face bobbling from a pulpit of stone.
Before the ceremony, we'd tossed in our pockets
of foreign coins—wishes aimed at his blind scowl.
Moonlight uprooting the slippery ribbon of his tail
while the current floated him,
floorboard by floorboard, across you & me.
A benediction in a sleeve of seawater,
the round polyp mouths of the reef opening like a choir.

Confluence

Daughter

*Like a mermaid in sea-weed, she dreams awake,
trembling in her soft and chilly nest.*
—John Keats

I first saw you in the soundwaves—
echoes sketching your nested bones.
Hadn't I prayed a rosary across each
buoy of your spine, your whorled
fingertips chalked in the amnion?

Out of the womb, you were wild in the sea.
Sign of the fish, you delighted in the brokenness
of the tide; its buoyant salt, an equilibrium
offering flight, tumbling buried things
into new hidden places. You loved seeds
and cocoons and homeless creatures
with shiny eyes and fangs. The natural world—

a simple hunger. Not like reading
the same primers the way the other students did,
or how you wrote in mirror images,
gleaning currents through an inverted lens.

You were born with an extra chain of lines
etched across the back of your pinky finger,
as if pricked by an odd luck spindle
that laced a red bead through your skin,
until an anger wormed into your artful bones.

You're tall now; your shadow longer than
most. You don't like to draw anymore—
the crayoned lines of your childhood
plucked into a bitter cantata, jawed down

to hard wax notes of indigo and aquamarine.
Even the word *sorrow* sounds like a color,
full of gristle and floodwater. Looking back,

I was wide-eyed the first time
the jellied wand found you curled
and hiccupping inside your little cove.
The whole horizon tilted to catch
your flickering heartbeat.
Still, I wonder, what did I miss?

The technician's room lit
with the labyrinth of the ultrasound
while I lay belly up, parsing
the rudiments like tea leaves—
interpretation of a dark concordance,
daughter, that could have been
you, that could have been me.

Were They Skates or Rays?

Were they skates or rays? God, I don't know.
Both, spineless things, which left
their whole bodies free to undulate as they circled
during the most vicious panic attack I've ever had—
chaperoning a first-grade field trip to Sea World.
People swarmed, masked in sweaty tourist mode,
or was I masked in a surface calm between
the penguins, the slap-happy tails of killer whales,
the dolphins grinning like flirty oceanic dogs.
The piped-in sound of a tide grounding itself
inside my skull until I'd wanted to run underwater
toward the nearest exit, my lungs spent
and releasing the core of me at last, broken
bubble-thin, a simple iridescence, please, God,
but I'd held to the rim and watched them instead—
the skates or the rays roiling in their pool
and brushing the reaching hands of the curious.
From inside the spinning current, I wondered
at the naked smoothness of their dark wings.

The Mermaid Who Loves Land Animals

In the water our daughter flits
and shimmies like a kite in wind,
long limbs aquatic as any iridescent tail.

*Your great-grandmother swam
the English Channel, came in second,*
her father tells her again,
as if she needed reminding
of her Viking heritage—
the balsa of her bone marrow,
the ice in her chromosomes.
Sea nymph with a scowl, butterfly

is her best stroke, but she prefers earth,
the apple snails beneath the bridge,
the humid air of antique marts
where skittish geckos glisten
on whalebone, walnut, hairpin lace.

She hypnotizes anole lizards,
clamps one on each earlobe,
sleeps with her fingers in nests
of speckled eggs and frog ponds—
an animal encyclopedia open at her bedside.
She will pour through it in the morning.

Her Danish relatives tell her
about the statue of the Little Mermaid
in Copenhagen Harbor—*"Den Lille Havfrue,"*
the girl who gave her tongue
for a pair of legs, who never swam
without wanting to walk upright in the sun.

Her pink mouth forming wishes
on every silver coin of moon.
Beads of air scoring the water skin—
ripple after ripple, soft as feathers or fur.

On Saturday Nights She Dances Alone in her Room—the Walls, a Shade of Blue-Green Called *Belize*

Zebra striped rug, a catch-all for lint and spinning,
her antique mirror quivering with techno bass.
On her dresser, a palette of eye shadow and lip gloss
hinges open like a keyboard. At twelve,
she plays at being a woman, trails her fingers
across the iridescence, is pinioned on high notes

of pumps borrowed from her mother's closet.
She collects Mardi Gras masks, plumes and sequins,
wraps her Barbie doll minions in duct tape miniskirts.
Her paintings whisper a different story—
shell pink heart with angel wings, sunflowers
in an Earth-shaped vase, and her mother's favorite—
freefalling leaves and feathers, a riotous migration.

In the morning, her mother gathers a trail
of eggshells and apple cores, watches the birds
outside her daughter's window and wonders why
God gifted them with both song and flight,
despite such tender, hollow bones.
Her nested princess wearing ebony gloss
on her toenails and fearing no ocean.
The blue jay opening its wings
to the morning like a black-tipped flower.

A Prayer for Those at the Edge of the Road

Sorrento, Florida

A woman holds up a sign
in front of the mower repair shop,
letting those of us in traffic know

she is homeless. Laborers
from the orchards and greenhouses
pause in their trucks to read

her face, resolute in the sharp
evening light of summer.
Her long, white dress floating

above the oily pavement,
is a mist by the time I pass
the nurseries. Orchids,

peace lilies, African violets
coved in a filmy, humid sky.
I wonder later if anyone stopped for her

when two girls at a gas station
in the city ask me to drive them home,
their baby blue eyes petaled in black

mascara. On this night of stranded women,
the moon is harsh and the nurseries
pulse with the silently broken

open. I meant to whisper a prayer
for those at the edge
of the road but I am distracted

with gravel and diesel and orchids,
and all the cruel possibilities weighed
between the roaring stars of headlights,

when I see a mother dog lolling
in the weeds at the shoulder of the road
with her baby, her soft, wild baby.

Trampolining

for Julia, the girl in the picture

I've caught her in mid-air,
                                       what's left
       of summer—
                          loose gold in an upsurge
of hair,
        a scalp-bounced, tree-ward,
    throng drawn
                 all the way
from her soles
              against the snap-back,
      shallow give
                of backyard earth,
stretched spring
            to spring,
   then trampolining up
                    & out.
Her mouth, a tunnel—
                    mid-word gone
    dark, bliss
             at the corner of her
lips, just an upswing,
              an almost
    exhale. One eye
               hidden in the reverb
of tangled bangs,
           the other caught
    like the wing-arc
             of a coasting bird,
a caged gaze,
        a defiance,
               a dare.
    Kinetic.
        No netting necessary.

Hannah

in memory

I'd heard about you before you became
my daughter's friend at the Christian school.
You were the girl, buoyant and uncombed,
with just a can of soup at the lunch table
and no way to open it, a name on a list
of a family asking for Christmas presents,
a wicked chant honed to the jump rope's beat.

I snickered at your clever nicknames for the pious,
the cartoon of our pastor blah-blah-blahing,
and yet, I'd wanted to complain to the same ones
about your influence on my daughter.
The two of you flipping your plaid Bible skirts
at the adolescent boys playing soccer; the pages
of their spiral notebooks licked damp with turning,
hearts & flowers sketched in the margins of yours.

The last time I saw you, you'd thrown yourself
fully clothed into a swimming pool amid
indignant snowbirds in a hotel downtown
and were led away dripping, a raspy sea siren.
You'd had babies early, lost them in a ruling,
wandered cowlicked, inked, and dimpled
down the highway toward Daytona Beach,
where you died, a stripper living in a van.

The final photo you posted was of a manakin
in white fishnets and a wolf mask, a macabre
piece of art meant to affront what terrified you.
A red jellyfish scribbled where the heart
might have been, skirted in smarting veins.

A third eye vortexed in onyx
across the flat plane of the plastic belly.

I wish I could have told you that
sometimes, Hannah, if we are just a body,
not somebody, just a body,
maybe it doesn't hurt so much.
That giddy smile of yours studded
in hard spangles, the lobes of your ears
opened wide as the well of a spoon.

I wish I could have taken you in, Hannah,
pushed you skyward
on the tire swing in our cul-de-sac,
filled your pockets with things girls should have—
birthstone charms & lullabies, a box of recipes.
The horizon, a tidy quilt of suburban green.

I wish I could have fanned that hard spark in you
into something more than what would consume
you. Your skin, a span of moonlight.
Stars lashing themselves against
the metal room of your van.
Earth's infinite spin, warm and quaking
the palm fronds like a loose spirit.

Missing the Missing Girl

i.
There's a lullaby in the cadence of streetlamps.
Night, a bulking thing. Did you hear her
speak about ghosts on the highway,
sorrows she could intuit through the walls
of cities she echoed past?
I think about her barking heart.
How it scratches at doors.
How it hears what others cannot.

ii.
Her lungs, we came to believe later,
were an anomaly—a pair of wings
inverted, stuffed inside a cage
of bone and stunted beneath
the lolling weight of the heart.

iii.
Charms. Look for what might have been
jostled from its jump ring—
that's what they call the dangle
from a clasp, where small stories ache
like muffled bells. As a girl, hadn't she loved
flowers, the ripe ones curled inside-out
and already nudged from their stems?

iv.
We're all an opening, honey,
someone says at a crosswalk
to a woman hurrying through the night.
The glass plane of my window,
sealed inside its watertight channel.

v.
We hope she's let her angels drive.
All she owns— a winter-thin bird
in a jar riding shotgun, and a cigarette
burn on a map where the compass rose had been.
We hope she's somewhere eating honey,
cursing her bee-stung fingers,
or searching for God, the soft planes
of him shaken out in the wind.

vi.
Someone says a group of kites
is called a mockery.
It is me, standing here on earth.
The strongest part of my body—
my calves, weighted and gleaming.
Isn't what's so fragile, so audacious,
meant to be airborne? A woman
reading on the porch of her
pretentious beach house
asks us to stop flying
our kites. Too distracting,
she says, squinting upward.

vii.
Hypnotic is what you might call
the impulse, girls. Lodestone
to the blood's briny metals.
Nothing shiny, tick-tocking
you into a trance. Nothing sensate
going slack at the roots of your molars.
Tongue, a crude fruit. Go deeper
into the brain's weeping
glands. Hormones— tripwires
in your innards; instinct, primal
as the amygdala's charge:
What'll it be tonight, darling,
fight or flight?

viii.
Run, honey, run,
someone says to a woman at a crosswalk,
Run before the light changes.

Vespers

Woman Struck by Lightning during Surprise Marriage Proposal

Max Patch Bald Mountain—Madison County, North Carolina

Some people climb there just for the stars—
a satiation in a sky so close the clouds,
silky and damp, slip right through you.
As for the view, there is no valley,
only a horizon of mountains fallen
open into a panorama of more—

Unakas, Smokies, Balsams and Black.
Ridges that lose color with distance,
silhouettes of undulations visible for miles.
Savage is a beautiful word, don't you think?
Like sweetbrier or glissando—
the way the bruising cloudbank skimmed
its shadow across the summit, blade by blade.

The lovers ascended the path undaunted.
Thunder quivering in the mayapples,
sun breaking through with the oddest moment
of brilliant illumination before he'd lain
backwards on the trail, his soles smoking,
diamond ring, a thin-lipped O singed into his hip.

Hadn't she meant to straddle two states that day—
North Carolina and Tennessee divided by a crest
of inclines that lumbered upwards, but what
did she mean just before she died when she said,
God, Baby, look how beautiful it is.

Sixteen Miles from Buffalo, Wyoming

The word *wing* opens into *Wyoming*—
a landscape of wind and sky,
where black cottonwoods loosen
with shredded cloud. An ancient sea
left these undulations in the horizon,
tucked fossils into the sandy hemline
of the Bighorn Mountains.

Ravaged remnants, scarp and shadow.
Elements that burn with ten thousand years
of winter. This summer solstice—
a startling of wildflowers,
the torque of river rush melded
with glaciers' snowy veins.
We climb horses like hills—
nub and sheen, June rising warm
beneath tooled leather, windblown
manes, lavender-scented sagebrush.

We hear there's a ghost in the ranch house
where we're staying and wonder why
she can't find her way out.
Maybe it's the continuum of one vastness
into another. This blue ocean of sky,
fathomless and riveting to its earthen floor
more than shell and bone, but spirits
burdened beyond hardships of season,
solitude, the howl of hunger—
every longing resonant with ponderous space.

A Walk through the Neighborhood before Nightfall

I am breath and ghost, not of these houses—
cozy dioramas swung shut, but not leveraged
enough by fences or lamplight that I can't
smell something delectable on your grill, neighbor.

I long for your perspective, to stand in your window
looking out, to carry the scent of your home in my hair.
Did I tell you I once saw a fox by that bridge?
From here, those cypress trees sway as tall as flagships.
How did you perfect that razored scallop in your hedge?

We share constellations and windchimes, the same
sparrows at the feeder. Clouds. Pollen. Potholes.
Not to mention this particular dimension of time
and space. Before we get too deep, let me
rearrange your spice rack, help you find your sandals,
linger with you over that jigsaw puzzle
on the dining room table. You'll laugh
when I tell you I once received an empty fortune
cookie before boarding a plane. I'm wayward,

too, you'll confide. From these shadows,
I can almost hear the dinner dishes being rinsed
in the sink and read like braille the coins
beneath the cushions of your sofa.
Let's light the candles, drink the wine.
Open the long jar of olives.
You see, your old dog loves me.
But don't worry, I'll be gone in the morning.
What a nice girl she was,
you'll remark over coffee and rye toast,
and no one will be able to remember my name.

Coyotes

Lying in bed next to me,
you didn't hear them last night.
Through our open window,
their hunger, loose & bristled.
It was a mournful oath taken
for what burrows wall-eyed
and unaware in its own
blood & marrow. The moon,

a distant fugue rolling off
those feral tongues
& spinning over rooftops,
knocking through thickets,
widening across highways
bent into sighs.
Didn't you feel it?

My veins scored open
on a howled point of gravity.
It's like this—when a woman
leans through darkness,
lips pursed & ready

at the candle's liquid rim,
it's the same sound the flame
would make before it goes out,
if it could, if it had more than

a wisp thin throat, its own
singular craven heat. *Solidarity,*
she would whisper back
to the smoke, into the sulky,
wanton dissipation, as if
there was a kinship there,
still jawed and pining.

Déjà Vu

There has to be darkness and a highway.
Beyond the shoulders of the road,
a topography lit in streetlamps.
You're seventeen, and if you look closely,

you can see the silhouette
of mountains beyond your reflection
in the car window. To the right, an anchor
store in a strip mall. To the left,
the gas station where high school boys work—

the good-looking ones who sweep the silk
of their long bangs from their eyes
with puppy-soft hands and ask if you want
regular or unleaded. Watching them comb
your windshield clean beneath
the squeegee's wide, forgiving blade,
you whisper: *Save me,*
and wonder, *does anyone do that anymore?*—

the windshield washing, you mean, of course,
and you know that if you slid your fingers
inside the thick baffles of their goose-down vests,
down into the warmth beneath
their soft-as-ash flannel shirts, your palms
would smell like gasoline and their father's
Old Spice, and that in the star bristled night,

every imagined kiss was a curfew, exquisitely unfair,
and a promise you had made in a fever to return
home what you'd borrowed just the way you found it.

Skinny Dipping in the Ocean at Age Fifty

Dancing was something we hadn't done in years,
we told one another that night, the three of us
marveling at our neon auras, fingers snapping,
cupping the cool walls of our cocktails, mid-spin.

Between us, eight children, seven husbands, fifteen
decades. In the air, a rhythm sparked and caught,
snippets of radiance scattered from the sphere
spinning above our heads. Didn't we deserve this,

to wring ourselves dizzy, to whip in the raw air,
to be this grateful, this forgiven? When the bar closed,
we'd drained our candy-colored drinks, bypassed
the palm trees admonishing with wind, the porch lights
of quiet pastel houses. We took the soft track of the beach
back to the rental, until one of us suggested jumping in.

We left our clothes in the sand, still warm
with the scent of us, as we toppled in, flapping angels
into the foamy drifts, howling our pact with the dark
and panting current, craving its ferocious kiss.

The last bits of us in lace and underwire, unhooked,
leafed from wet skin, then flung across the broken sea,
while our daughters waiting on the shore wondered
at the hour and combed their siren-silky hair.

Meet my Anxiety

I really didn't want you to see it
this way, to have to acknowledge
the flicker of repulsion, some kind
of gratitude in your wide, soft eyes.
Don't stare too hard at what should be
pickled in a jar of formaldehyde,
the ganglia of nerve endings,
the fetus face of perpetual shriek.

You've caught me naked.
Let me try to explain. You see,
it is my parasitic twin, my would-be
circus act of grotesque proportion,
the partial eclipse at my solar plexus.
Portable as a papoose, I carry it
everywhere. If you could only lift
the vestment of my skin, part the blood
I share like mother's milk,
you'd understand: *I do not travel lightly.*

But don't worry, it will sleep for months—
a twitching fit of hibernation, dreams
so thick it sinks smoothly under,
but when it surfaces, Oh God, it reeks
of dead things and rails so ravenously
I'll gasp midsentence, startle into a run
hard enough to rattle the incessant clawing,
the squat tongue sucking marrow.

Its hunger keeps me up at night.
Colic was a breeze. I rock
in waking daydreams. My brain clamps
with rhythmic wailing, pre-dawn ticks
of clocks. My palms too slippery to hold
it in. Okay, scalpels of surgeons have dislodged
sticky membranes of me in the past—
tonsil and tumor, but this thing shares my breath.
In a panic, I'll bolt from Walmart again,
the line at the bank, your invitation to brunch.
Can you see why I don't stand too close?

Heart

i.
In the beginning that's all there is—
   a loose knot spun
   from a cellular script,
       tweaked to trill.
First red, a feathery font inside
the translucent seahorse-shaped fetus.

ii.
Queen bee, nursing mother
anchored into the blue-red mouths
of twins—aorta and vena cava.
The body's ocean of famishment,
a spent child hiccupping tears.
Rhythm of a lullaby in a rocking chair:
hush-hush, Moonbeam, hush-hush.

iii.
A boy once gave me
his Saint Christopher medal—
a proclamation as aqua blue
as the neighborhood pool
where he asked for it back a week later.
Pressed to the wall between
my preadolescent breasts,
my heart was an eavesdropper
that had leaned in and borrowed
the blue extravagance like an eye.

iv.
They say the heart can transplant
its cravings into another's body
when stitched inside
like a slippery mollusk,
tonguing its way around.
What would mine bring—
a penchant for brash, dark-eyed men,
a phobia of lightning and bridges,
the same sentient dreams?

v.
It is said there are four rooms
in the heart and just one cadence.
I say it's a kaleidoscope
of tilt and geometry and glass,
with a portal too small
for your eye to see kites
being jostled on their strings,
the star points and ink strokes,
the origami folds of mirror and sky.

vi.
No one has ever seen my heart,
I want to tell him, this stranger
sculpting forms with sound waves
beneath my jellied sternum.
The conversation is casual,
as if he'd traced the outline
of a woman's heart many times before,

known its singular creature-beat
unshelled into the sterile room.
I turn my head away from my heart,
in its aquarium of still frames,
blooming and closing so rapidly
at the glass wall, he tells me
he knows I am afraid.

Urchin

Between the shiny rings
of tide, a flower—
sudden and unexpected.
A bone-colored
chrysanthemum,
midsummer.
Her fingers crumble
its textures,
like an ocean, like a hunger
succinct in a bucket's
bright plastic well,
where the moon will skim
this pooled bit of night
in increments of a bloom wilting—
tentacles falling away like thistle,
and a bald pod beneath,
hollowed by morning,
that still whispers of surfaces:
sea foam, aqua, stars.

Floating Past the Orange House in Amalfi

I'd take that one
perched by itself between
the cleave-on-cleave
of ocean & cypress & limestone.

As a girl, hadn't I drawn mountains
by tracing my splayed fingers
across notebook paper,
a geography overstated
in its remoteness,
like the way I'd seen islands
in that inkblot test, a sense of isolation
noted in the margins
by the assessor in his wide tie
and moccasins, but not loneliness,
I would have told him, not loneliness.

From that distance, nothing
could surprise me
at the door of the orange house,
I mean. No guest arriving
without me having time
to drop a splay of lilies
into a blue vase, light the candles,
let the butter soften for the bread.
There would be a dog or two,
of course, that would wake
and sniff the salt air,
stretch a sigh from their limbs.
And I'd grow a garden—
plum tomatoes, rosemary, fragile leaves
of arugula, a trellis of grapes.

From that distance, nothing
but orange walls changing hues in the light,
news that would arrive civilly rolled in paper,
or on a postcard of foreign stamps.
From that distance, nothing,
but clouds, cool & damp,
nosing at the lace curtains.
A featherbed. A fireplace.
A tree bent with Caravaggio lemons.
From that distance, nothing
wounded or loose, hungry or thronging,
but the cool blue industry of the sea.

She Speaks in Maps

If you say the word *north*
or *landmark, coastline,* or *detour,*
my mother will grab her map
and unfold the globe for you in a jigsaw
of plats. Latitudes and longitudes—
those creases where well-worn highways
connect and diverge. A compass rose
pressed in every ocean. We tell her

she must have been a navigator
in a previous life, knowing the way
she likes a satellite view on possibility,
remembering how she'd left behind
a letter for each of us the first time
she'd flown away. There were postcards—

Kenya and the Amalfi coast, Norway
with its lacy fjords carved by glacier fingers,
Singapore & Patagonia, Bora Bora & Peru.
In Spain, someone had stolen her purse.
While sailing, she'd seen the Amazon
merge in striations of coffee and cream,
followed the Nile's narrow emerald valley,
hiked China's Great Wall—an antiquity
whose windings can be seen from space.

And now at eighty, on the west coast
of Florida, she's decided she is wild
about the nature of the subtropical sky.
Is it enough to be awed by its unpredictability?
Diorama of cloud and wind, heat
lightning silently sparking, the evolution
of topography in every cumulus ridge.

She joins the beachgoers on the shore
in the last illuminant hour of day
to watch sun and ocean merge—
a line as red as a highway on a map,
paralleling the vast, liquid edge.

About the Author

Laura Sobbott Ross has worked as a teacher and a writing coach in Lake County, Florida, where she was named as the inaugural poet laureate. Her poetry appears in many journals, including *32 Poems, Blackbird,* and the *Florida Review.* She was a finalist for the Arts&Letters Poetry Award and won the Southern Humanities Review Auburn Witness Poetry Prize. She's the author of two chapbooks and three poetry books.

www.ingramcontent.com/pod-product-compliance
Lightning Source LLC
Chambersburg PA
CBHW032233080426
42735CB00008B/833